Usborne

Things to Spot
in
LONDON
STICKER BOOK

Rob Lloyd Jones

Illustrated by Carlo Stanga

Tower Bridge

Buckingham Palace

London Transport

Tower Bridge

With its distinctive stone towers, Tower Bridge is one of London's most famous landmarks. Completed in 1894, it remains the only bridge over the River Thames that opens in the middle. The bridge has two sections (called bascules) that rise up to let tall ships pass through. This happens around 1,000 times a year.

In 1977, Tower Bridge was painted red, white and blue to celebrate the Queen's Silver Jubilee.

Look out for... the Victorian engine rooms and the high walkways that connect the two towers. The walkways hold regular exhibitions and have stunning views of the river, 42m (138ft) below.

Buckingham Palace

Buit in 1705, this enormous house became the official home of British kings and queens when Queen Victoria came to the throne in 1837. With almost 800 rooms, including 52 bedrooms, 78 bathrooms, a post office and cinema, the palace has over 600 members of staff, including two people to look after its 300 clocks.

Public tours take place in August and September. You can visit 19 beautiful State Rooms, where the Queen entertains guests, and part of the garden.

Look out for... the 'Changing the Guard' ceremony at 11:30 every morning, as new guards come on duty.

London Transport

London has the world's largest public transport system – around 6.5 million people travel around the city every day.

London's first double decker bus, introduced in 1829, was pulled by horses. There are now more than 700 different London bus routes, serviced by 7,500 buses.

The world's first underground train line opened in London in 1863. Today, the city has almost 300 underground stations – more than in any other city, and the tracks extend for 402km (249 miles).

You can also get about in black taxi cabs. If the orange 'TAXI' sign on top is lit up, it means the cab is available.

The Golden Hinde

This magnificent ship is a replica of a Tudor ship that sailed around the world from 1577 to 1580. The original ship's captain, Sir Francis Drake, wasn't just an explorer. He also attacked other ships, stealing chests of treasure and making a fortune for Queen Elizabeth I.

This replica ship has sailed over 225,000km (140,000 miles) – much further than the real *Golden Hinde* ever sailed.

Look out for... the golden 'hinde' (deer) on the ship's crest, symbol of Sir Christopher Hatton, who paid for Drake's voyage.

The Golden Hinde

Westminster Abbey

There has been an abbey on this site for over a thousand years. Most of the abbey you see today was built between the 13th and 16th centuries, except the two towers, completed in 1745, designed by architect Nicholas Hawksmoor.

Since 1066, all Britain's kings and queens have been crowned here. Most are buried here too, as well as many of the country's most famous writers, poets, scientists, generals, actors and politicians.

Look out for... the Coronation Chair and the wooden throne on which monarchs are crowned.

Westminster Abbey

Houses of Parliament

The Houses of Parliament, or Palace of Westminster, is where the government meets to make laws. Inside there are more than 5km (3 miles) of corridors and 1,100 rooms. The most famous is the House of Commons, where MPs debate, and Westminster Hall, the remains of a medieval palace that once stood here.

If a flag is flying at the top, it means the politicians are meeting inside.

Look out for... the famous Clock Tower. 'Big Ben' is the nickname of the huge bronze bell inside.

Houses of Parliament

St. James's Park

St. James's Park

Created in 1603 for James I, this is London's oldest royal park and one of the prettiest. It has a small lake with many birds, including swans and ducks.

From the bridge, there are views of Buckingham Palace and Horse Guards Parade, where traditional military ceremonies are held.

When the park was first built, exotic beasts such as camels, crocodiles and elephants were kept here to entertain the royal family. In the 18th century, cows grazed here and people came to buy fresh mugs of milk.

Look out for... the Great White Pelicans, fed at 2:30pm every day.

The Monument

The tallest free-standing stone column in the world, the Monument was built in 1677 to commemorate the Great Fire of London. The copper urn at the top symbolizes the flames. You can climb 311 winding stairs inside to reach the viewing platform at the top.

The Monument is 61.5m (203 ft) high – the distance from its base to the spot where the fire broke out – at a bakery in Pudding Lane, on 2 September 1666.

Look out for... the sculptures on the base showing King Charles II as he makes plans to rebuild the city.

The Monument

Natural History Museum

This striking Victorian building contains a vast collection of animals, plants, rocks and fossils from all over the world. This includes a snarling model of a Tyrannosaurus rex, one of the world's biggest trees and a life-sized model of a blue whale.

The museum also has over 17 million insect specimens, including a new species discovered in 2007 in the museum's own garden.

Look out for... the spectacular new Darwin Centre, where you can watch scientists in action studying plants and animals.

Natural History Museum

The London Eye

This huge wheel was built on the South Bank of the River Thames to celebrate the new millennium in 2000, but was so popular it became permanent. It's 135m (450ft) high – three times higher than Tower Bridge – and has a diameter of 120m (393ft). Each passenger capsule takes about 30 minutes to go all the way around. Passengers can step on and off without the wheel stopping.

Look out for... spectacular views of London from the top. On a clear day, you can see for over 40km (25 miles), all the way to Windsor Castle.

The London Eye

30, St. Mary Axe

30, St. Mary Axe

The proper name of this glass building is 30, St. Mary Axe, but it's known as 'the Gherkin' because of its unusual shape. Designed by Norman Foster, it's 180m (590ft) high, and has 40 floors of offices. When it was built, the grave of a teenage Roman girl was discovered buried underneath. It's still there now.

Look out for... the dark shades of glass, which create a spiral pattern. The outside is made up of 7,429 panes of glass – enough to cover five football fields. Every pane is flat, except one – the piece at the top.

No. 10, Downing Street

This famous address has been the home of British prime ministers since 1735. It's actually three houses joined together, with over 100 rooms inside. They include elegant dining rooms, where visiting world leaders are entertained, the grand entrance hall with its striking black and white marble floor, and the Cabinet Room, where the Prime Minister meets his closest advisers.

No. 10, Downing Street was once owned by a man named Mr. Chicken.

Did you know... the famous front door looks as if it's made of wood, but in fact it's reinforced steel, to withstand terrorist attacks.

City Hall

This unusually shaped glass building is where the Mayor of London works. It has ten floors of offices and holds regular exhibitions about London. There is a platform at the top with views up and down the River Thames.

The building was designed by Norman Foster, cost £43 million to construct, and is made of 4,000 tons of steel and glass.

Notice... its strange, lopsided shape. Some people say it looks like an onion, or a motorcycle helmet. What do you think?

Marble Arch

This imposing stone archway was built as the main entrance to Buckingham Palace in 1828. Later, it was taken away and put in its current position at the bottom of Oxford Street, and used as a police station until 1950. It contains three rooms, one on each side of the arch and another across the top.

As a royal gateway, it is officially illegal for anyone except the Royal Family and royal guards to pass through. But everyone does.

Look out for... a plaque on the ground that marks the spot where public executions used to take place. Around 50,000 criminals were hanged here, between 1300 and 1783.

No. 10, Downing Street

City Hall

Marble Arch

Albert Memorial

Queen Victoria ordered this extravagant monument to be built in memory of her husband, Prince Albert. The statue of the Prince is covered in glimmering gold leaf, surrounded by an ornate roof with mosaics of angels, and a gold cross on the top. Sculptures on the memorial represent the different continents.

Prince Albert said he didn't want a statue, but Queen Victoria obviously didn't listen.

Look out for... the marble frieze around the base. It shows 169 life-size sculptures of poets, painters, architects and composers.

Albert Memorial

St. James's Palace

St. James's Palace

Built in the 1530s, St. James's Palace was the main residence of the royal family for around 300 years. King Charles I spent his last night in the palace before being executed the next day. The palace includes luxury apartments, a chapel, dining halls and reception rooms.

It's also home to the oldest and most valuable stamp collection in the world, owned by the Queen.

Look out for... the imposing red-brick Tudor gatehouse. Most of the original Palace was damaged by a fire in 1809, except the gatehouse.

Cleopatra's Needle

Named after the ancient Egyptian queen Cleopatra, this 21m (68ft) high granite obelisk was a gift from the Egyptian government. It was brought to London in 1878 on a specially designed ship. Almost 3,500 years old, it is inscribed with hieroglyphs and surrounded by statues of mythical beasts called sphinxes.

There's a box buried beneath the obelisk containing items from the 1870s, including newspapers and coins.

Look out for... chips in the base of one of the sphinxes, caused by a bomb during the First World War.

Cleopatra's Needle

Tate Modern

This vast old power station has been transformed into one of London's largest and most popular art galleries. You'll find paintings, sculptures and photographs by the most famous artists from the past hundred years, including Pablo Picasso, Jackson Pollock, Salvador Dali and Andy Warhol.

The huge central hall, the Turbine Hall, used to contain electricity generators. The tower was the station's old chimney.

Look out for... the spectacular views from the top floor, up and down the River Thames.

Tate Modern

Shakespeare's Globe

Shakespeare's Globe is an almost perfect reconstruction of a playhouse that stood nearby over 300 years ago. Finished in 1987, it was built close to the original, with oak timbers, wooden pegs for nails, and the first thatched roof in central London since the 17th century (when they were banned in case of fires).

William Shakespeare was one of the owners of the original Globe. Several of his famous plays were first performed on its small wooden stage.

Look out for... the exhibition next door, where you can find out more about the Globe's history.

Shakespeare's Globe

The British Museum

Established in 1753, the British Museum is the oldest public museum in the world, with a vast collection, including ancient Egyptian mummies. At its heart is the glass-roofed Great Court, and a library, known as the Reading Room.

The famous Parthenon Marbles were taken from an Ancient Greek temple over 100 years ago. Today, the Greek government wants them back.

Look out for... a 5,000 year-old Egyptian body, so well preserved you can still see its ginger hair.

The British Museum

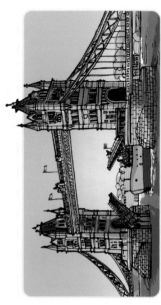

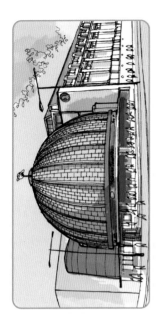

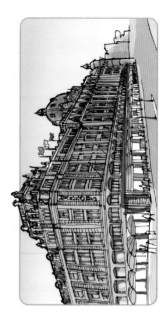

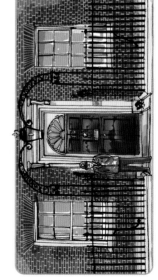

Lloyd's building

Home of the insurance company Lloyd's of London, this striking building was designed by architect Richard Rogers, and opened in 1986. It's nicknamed the 'inside-out building' because it has staircases, elevators and water pipes outside, to make more space for offices inside. There's an 18th century dining room inside, brought in, bit by bit, from the old Lloyd's building across the road.

Look out for... the small cranes on top of the building. These helped to build it, but were then kept in place as decoration.

Lloyd's Building

Kensington Gardens

Kensington Gardens

This elegant park was created in the 18th century for King William III, who lived at nearby Kensington Palace. Today the palace is more famously associated with Diana, Princess of Wales, who also lived there.

You can find a bronze statue of Peter Pan, whose magical adventures were partly set in the gardens. The design of the 'Sunken Garden' mirrors a garden at Hampton Court Palace.

Look out for... a 900 year-old tree stump called 'Elfin Oak', carved to look as if tiny elves and gnomes are hiding inside its bark.

Gerrard Street

Decorated with red lanterns, stone lions, and brightly painted gates, Gerrard Street is at the heart of London's Chinese community, in an area known as Chinatown. Some of London's first Chinese people came here in the 18th century.

The street is known for its restaurants and shops selling Chinese goods that aren't available elsewhere. The most exciting time to visit is in Chinese New Year, in late January to mid February.

Look out for... street signs around Gerrard Street written in Mandarin, the main language of China.

Gerrard Street

Victoria and Albert Museum

Victoria and Albert Museum

The Victoria and Albert Museum (V&A) is London's leading museum of art and design. It contains over 4.5 million objects, including ceramics, sculpture, fashion, jewellery and furniture from all over the world.

The V&A owns the earliest photograph of London. Taken in 1839, it shows Trafalgar Square before Nelson's Column was built.

Look out for... Tipu's Tiger, an 18th century model of a tiger attacking a solider. Organ keys make the tiger growl and roar.

Westminster Cathedral

Completed in 1903, the headquarters of the Roman Catholic Church in Britain was built to look more like a Byzantine church than an English cathedral – with soaring domes and elegant towers. The walls and columns are made of over 100 different types of marble, and decorated with dazzling golden mosaics.

The cathedral was built on a site used for many things, including a market, a bull ring and a prison.

Look out for... the bell tower. You can climb the steps to see fantastic views of Buckingham Palace and the Houses of Parliament.

Westminster Cathedral

Bank of England

The Bank of England, set up in 1694, looks after the government's money. Its concrete-lined vaults contain around 300,000 solid gold bars, worth over £73 billion. In its museum, you can lift a real gold bar, and see weapons once used to defend the Bank from thieves.

The Bank is nicknamed the 'Old Lady of Threadneedle Street', after the street it stands on.

Look out for... examples of every coin ever made in Britain. You can also see a reconstruction of a typical bank office, dating from 1790.

Bank of England

Trafalgar Square

This famous square was built to celebrate an important naval victory at the Battle of Trafalgar in 1805. In the middle is Nelson's Column, topped with a statue of Admiral Lord Nelson, who led the British fleet.

Today the Square is a popular place for national celebrations, political rallies and displays of modern art. More than 15 million people visit each year, making it the world's fourth most popular tourist site.

Look out for... the four bronze lions at the bottom, called Landseer's Lions, after the artist who designed them. They're made from melted down cannons of old battleships.

Trafalgar Square

London Zoo

London Zoo first opened in 1828. Today, its main concern is with conservation projects to protect endangered species around the world. There are over 10,000 animals, from around 700 different species. Zoo keepers are happy to tell you more about how they look after the penguins and the other animals. The most popular animals include tigers, lions, gorillas, giraffes, giant tortoises and Komodo dragons.

Look out for... feeding time at the penguin pool, every day from 1.30pm.

London Zoo

St. Paul's Cathedral

The soaring dome of St. Paul's Cathedral is one of the most famous landmarks in the world. Inside, it's decorated with intricate wooden carvings and mosaics. You can climb up the dome too. It's 550 steps to the Golden Gallery at the very top, where you get stunning views across London.

Completed in 1710, it was designed by Sir Christopher Wren. Its 111 m (364ft) high dome is the second largest in Europe, after St. Peter's in Rome.

Look out for... the huge crypt. Among the famous people buried there are the Duke of Wellington and Admiral Lord Nelson.

St. Paul's Cathedral

National Gallery

The National Gallery is free to visit and there are over 2,300 paintings on display, including works by some of the most famous artists in the world, such as Michelangelo, Rembrandt, Vincent van Gogh and Monet.

During the Second World War, the collection was moved to a quarry in Wales, to protect it from air raids.

Look out for... Leonardo da Vinci's painting *The Virgin and Child with St. Anne and St. John the Baptist*. It hangs in a special darkened room to protect it from the light.

National Gallery

London: a brief history

Almost 2,000 years ago: Romans invaded Britain and built a town by the River Thames called Londinium.

By 200: Londinium was the biggest town in Britain, with a market, a military fort, and an arena for gladiator fights.

Around 400 - 1000: The Romans left. London was inhabited by Saxons, and later, Vikings.

1066: The Norman William the Conqueror invaded England. He built the Tower of London as his palace.

By 1300: London had grown into one of the world's biggest cities, with around 80,000 people. A terrible disease known as The Black Death spread quickly, killing thousands.

1400s: The city expanded. Many grand mansions, such as Banqueting House, were built.

1500s: King Henry VIII built St. James's Palace. St. James's Park was laid out as royal gardens. The *Golden Hinde* set sail from London's docks. Inns and playhouses lined the south bank.

1665-1666: The Great Plague, followed by the Great Fire of London

1700s: St. Paul's Cathedral, the Bank of England and the British Museum were built. London's population grew to one million.

1800s: London was the heart of the vast British empire. The riverbanks were crowded with factories, and the population boomed to six million.

1837: Queen Victoria moved into Buckingham Palace.

1840s: Building began on the Houses of Parliament.

1851: The Great Exhibition was held in Hyde Park to celebrate science and industry. The V&A and the Science Museums were built from its profits.

1863: The world's first underground train line opened in London. Steam trains brought thousands into the city.

1940s During the Second World War, the city was bombed in air raids known as the Blitz. The government met in underground Cabinet War Rooms.

London today: Around eight million people now live here. Striking new buildings have been built, such as 30, St. Mary Axe and City Hall.